CONTENTS

INTRODUCTION • *2*

QUILT INSTRUCTIONS:

Winter Star • *3*

Table Runner • *8*

Globes • *13*

Crystal Blue • *21*

Holiday Harlequin • *29*

Tree Skirt • *32*

ABOUT THE AUTHOR • *36*

INTRODUCTION

To be honest, I don't really care for winter. I like the sun, warmth, a nice tropical breeze… That being said, there is still something magical about the first snow of winter. The way the light reflects off all of those little crystals of ice, the change in the landscape as snow blankets the ground and clings to all the tree branches — it really can be a lovely time, and as long as I am inside, sitting by the fire, with a warm drink, looking out at it all, I can live with it. Though usually, as soon as it snows at our house, Zack has me outside and is pelting me with snowballs until I am frozen through — ah, fatherhood!

My inspiration for this book, and the Wintergraphix fabric collections, is definitely nature. I want to capture some of the wonder and excitement that winter brings. The patterns in this book celebrate winter more than they do a particular holiday — so, whatever holiday it is that you enjoy this time of year, hopefully the projects will help to decorate your home and create an environment full of beauty and joy.

Best Wishes for the Holidays,

—Jason Yenter

WINTER STAR

This is the most traditional pattern in the book. A simple star block mixed with "flying geese" creates a beautiful quilt in either the traditional red and green, or a slightly more contemporary blue and green.

Finished Quilt Size: 55½" x 55½"

Finished Star Block Size: 8" x 8"

See this quilt in color on the back cover and inside front cover.

Materials

Fabric requirements are based on 40" fabric width. *A separate materials list is given for each version of this quilt.*

Red Quilt

- 1⅓ yds. White Snowflake (8WG4) for blocks
- 1¼ yds. Red Filigree (4WGB1) for blocks
- 1 yd. Green Calligraphy (5FG24) for blocks and binding
- 1¼ yds. Red Holly Collage (1WGB1) for blocks, sashing, and inner border
- 1⅞ yds. Red Lace Stripe (3WGB1) for outer border
- 3¾ yds. for backing

Blue Quilt

- 1⅓ yds. White Snowflake (8WG4) for blocks
- 1¼ yds. Blue Filigree (4WGB2) for blocks
- 1 yd. Green Calligraphy (5FG24) for blocks and binding
- 1¼ yds. Blue Holly Collage (1WGB2) for blocks, sashing, and inner border
- 1⅞ yds. Blue Lace Stripe (3WGB2) for outer border
- 3¾ yds. for backing

Directions

All cutting measurements include ¼"-wide seam allowance. Unless otherwise indicated, cut strips across fabric width. Press seams in direction of arrows unless otherwise instructed.

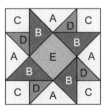

Star Block

Large Flying Geese Unit

Small Flying Geese Unit

Hourglass Block

16-patch Block

Cutting

One set of cutting instructions is given, to be used for either the Red Quilt or the Blue Quilt. Fabrics are cut in the order given in the Materials list.

From White Snowflake, cut:
- 32 squares, 5¼" x 5¼"; cut each square twice diagonally to make 128 of triangle A
- 64 squares, 2½" x 2½", for C squares

From Filigree, cut:
- 2 strips, 1½" x 40", for strip-piecing J squares
- 20 squares, 5¼" x 5¼"; cut each square twice diagonally to make 80 of triangle B
- 64 squares, 2⅞" x 2⅞"; cut each square once diagonally to make 128 of triangle F

From Green Calligraphy, cut:
- 6 strips, 2½" x 40", for double-fold binding
- 2 strips, 1½" x 40", for strip-piecing I squares
- 32 squares, 2⅞" x 2⅞"; cut each square once diagonally to make 64 of triangle D

From Holly Collage, cut:
- 8 rectangles, 4½" x 8½", for sashing
- 4 rectangles, 2½" x 20½", for inner border
- 4 rectangles, 2½" x 10½", for inner border
- 4 rectangles, 2½" x 8½", for inner border
- 2 squares, 5¼" x 5¼"; cut each square twice diagonally to make 8 of triangle G
- 8 squares, 2⅞" x 2⅞"; cut each square once diagonally to make 16 of triangle H
- 16 squares, 3⅜" x 3⅜", for E squares

From Lace Stripe, cut:
- 4 strips, 4" x length of fabric, for outer border (*Note:* Selectively cut border strips so that the design is the same in each strip, as shown in the photos on the back cover and inside front cover; this will make the design match at the mitered corners.)

Block Assembly

1. Using these pieces:
   1 Holly Collage E square
   4 Filigree B triangles
   4 Green Calligraphy D triangles
   4 White Snowflake A triangles
   4 White Snowflake C squares
   …assemble a Star block as shown. Repeat to make a total of 16 blocks.

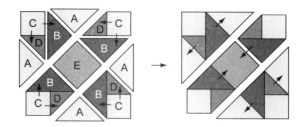

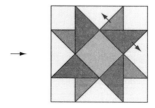

Make 16.

2. Using 4 White Snowflake A triangles and 8 Filigree F triangles, assemble a Large Flying Geese unit. Repeat to make a total of 16 units.

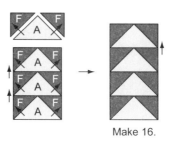

Make 16.

3. Using 1 Filigree B triangle and 2 Holly Collage H triangles, assemble a Small Flying Geese unit. Repeat to make a total of 8 units.

Make 8.

4. Using 2 Filigree B triangles and 2 Holly Collage G triangles, assemble an Hourglass block. Repeat to make a total of 4 blocks.

Make 4.

5. Using 2 Filigree 1½" strips, and 2 Green Calligraphy 1½" strips, assemble an I/J/I/J strip unit as shown. From the strip unit, cut a total of 20 I/J/I/J segments, each 1½" wide.

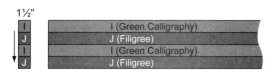

Make 1 strip unit.
Cut 20 segments.

6. Using 4 I/J/I/J segments, assemble a 16-patch block as shown. Repeat to make a total of 5 blocks.

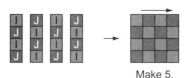

Make 5.

Quilt Top Assembly

1. Sew together in a horizontal row: 4 Star blocks, 2 Large Flying Geese units, and 1 Holly Collage 4½" x 8½" rectangle. (Make sure that the Large Flying Geese units are oriented as shown.) Repeat to make a total of 4 rows.

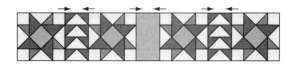

Make 4.

2. Sew together in a horizontal row: 4 Large Flying Geese units, two 16-patch blocks, and 1 Hourglass block. (Make sure that the Large Flying Geese units are oriented as shown.) Repeat to make a total of 2 rows.

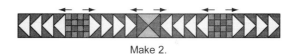

Make 2.

3. Sew together in a horizontal row: 4 Holly Collage 4½" x 8½" rectangles, 2 Hourglass blocks, and one 16-patch block.

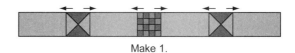

Make 1.

4. Sew together the horizontal rows made in Quilt Top Assembly Steps 1-3 on page 5. Make sure that the rows are oriented as shown below.

Borders

1. For side inner borders, sew together in a horizontal row: 2 Holly Collage 2½" x 8½" rectangles, 2 Small Flying Geese units, and 1 Holly Collage 2½" x 20½" rectangle. Repeat to make a total of 2 rows.

Make 2.

Following placement shown in the Quilt Diagram on page 7, sew rows to sides of quilt. Press seams toward borders.

2. For top and bottom inner borders, sew together in a horizontal row: 2 Holly Collage 2½" x 10½" rectangles, 2 Small Flying Geese units, and 1 Holly Collage 2½" x 20½" rectangle. Repeat to make a total of 2 rows.

Make 2.

Sew rows to top and bottom of quilt as shown in the Quilt Diagram. Press seams toward borders.

3. For mitered outer borders: with right sides together, pin 2 Lace Stripe strips to sides of quilt top (border strips should extend approximately equally beyond top and bottom of quilt; it's easiest if you start pinning at the center of the border and work outward). Sew, beginning and ending ¼" from raw edges of quilt top, as shown. Backstitch to secure. Press seams toward borders.

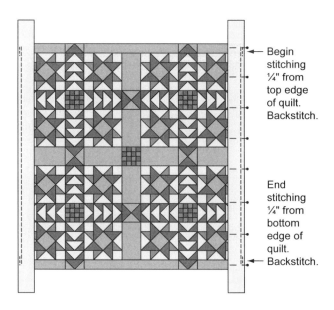

Begin stitching ¼" from top edge of quilt. Backstitch.

End stitching ¼" from bottom edge of quilt. Backstitch.

4. Repeat Step 3 with top and bottom borders, starting and ending stitching ¼" from side edges of quilt top (backstitch to secure), being careful not to catch side borders in seams.

5. Working on a table, fold quilt top so that borders at one corner of the quilt are aligned, with right sides together and raw edges even. (For this step, fold the pressed seam allowances back toward the quilt top.) Pin borders together as shown below. Use a ruler and a sharp pencil to draw a stitching line on wrong side of border. (Align long edge of ruler with folded edge of quilt top, and align 45° line on ruler with border edges.) The drawn line should begin where the border stitching ends, and the drawn line should end at the border edges.

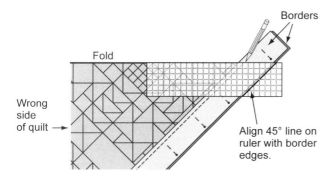

6. Pin over drawn line, through both borders, to secure; then stitch on the drawn line, beginning at inner corner with backstitch, and ending at border outer raw edges. Trim excess, leaving a ¼"-wide seam allowance.

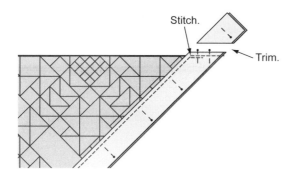

7. Press corner seam open.

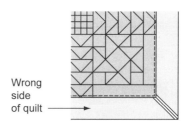

8. Repeat Steps 5-7 with remaining three corners of quilt top. Press border seams back down toward borders.

Finishing

Layer quilt top, batting, and backing. Quilt as desired. Sew binding using your favorite method. Don't forget to sign and date your finished quilt.

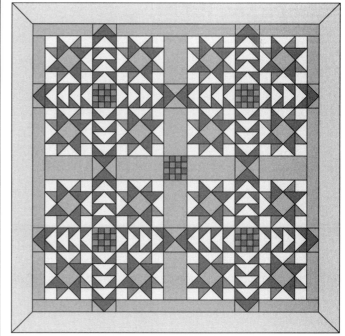

Quilt Diagram

TABLE RUNNER

I love to set a beautiful table that my family can gather around for a special holiday dinner. This table runner will be a lovely base for your table, and would look wonderful with coordinated napkins made from one of the featured prints.

Finished Table Runner
Size: 14" x 52"

Finished Block Size: 8" x 8"

See this project in color in the center section of the book.

Materials

Fabric requirements are based on 40" fabric width.

- ⅜ yd. White Snowflake (8WG4) for blocks
- ¾ yd. Red Filigree (4WGB1) for blocks, outer border, and binding
- ⅓ yd. Green Calligraphy (5FG24) for blocks and inner border
- ½ yd. Red Holly Collage (1WGB1) for blocks and setting triangles
- 1⅞ yds. for backing

Directions

All cutting measurements include ¼"-wide seam allowance. Unless otherwise indicated, cut strips across fabric width. Press seams in direction of arrows unless otherwise instructed.

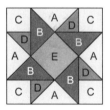

Star Block

Cutting

From White Snowflake, cut:
- 4 squares, 5¼" x 5¼"; cut each square twice diagonally to make 16 of triangle A
- 16 squares, 2½" x 2½", for C squares

From Red Filigree, cut:
- 4 strips, 2½" x 40", for double-fold binding
- 2 strips, 1" x 40", for outer border
- 2 rectangles, 1½" x 11", for outer border
- 2 rectangles, 1½" x 10", for outer border
- 4 squares, 5¼" x 5¼"; cut each square twice diagonally to make 16 of triangle B

From Green Calligraphy, cut:
- 2 strips, 1" x 40", for inner border
- 2 rectangles, 1½" x 10", for inner border
- 2 rectangles, 1½" x 9", for inner border
- 8 squares, 2⅞" x 2⅞"; cut each square once diagonally to make 16 of triangle D

From Red Holly Collage, cut:
- 2 squares, 12⅝" x 12⅝"; cut each square twice diagonally to make 8 setting triangles (2 extra)
- 4 squares, 3⅜" x 3⅜", for E squares

Assembly

1. Using these pieces:
   1 Red Holly Collage E square
   4 Red Filigree B triangles
   4 Green Calligraphy D triangles
   4 White Snowflake A triangles
   4 White Snowflake C squares
   …assemble a Star block as shown. Repeat to make a total of 4 blocks.

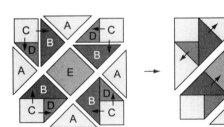

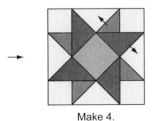

Make 4.

2. Sew blocks and Red Holly Collage setting triangles together in rows as shown.

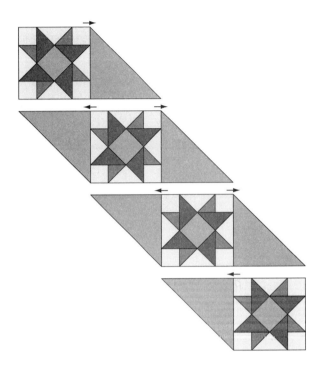

3. Sew rows together. Press seams in one direction.

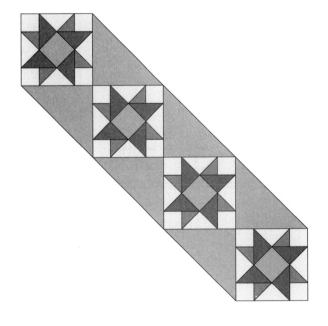

Borders

1. Sew 1 Green Calligraphy 1½" x 9" rectangle to each end of table runner as shown. Press seams toward rectangles. Then add 1 Green Calligraphy 1½" x 10" rectangle to each end of table runner. Press seams toward rectangles just added.

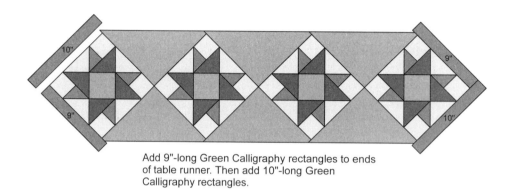

Add 9"-long Green Calligraphy rectangles to ends of table runner. Then add 10"-long Green Calligraphy rectangles.

2. Using an acrylic ruler and rotary cutter – and aligning the long edge of the ruler with the long edge of the table runner, and also aligning the 45° line on the ruler with the edge of the rectangle as shown – trim the overhanging end of each rectangle.

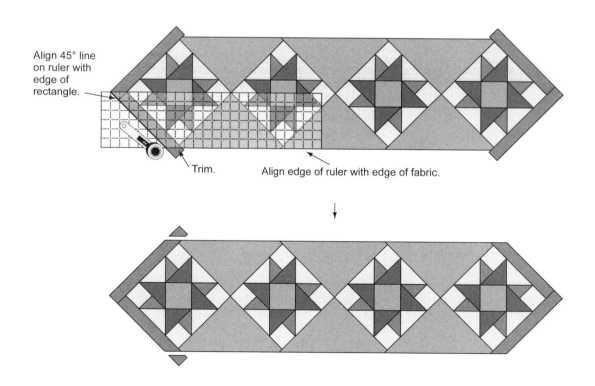

Align 45° line on ruler with edge of rectangle.

Trim.

Align edge of ruler with edge of fabric.

3. With right sides together, pin 1 Green Calligraphy 1" x 40" inner border strip to each long side of the table runner. (Border strips should extend approximately equally beyond each side of table runner; it's easiest if you start pinning at the center of the strip and work outward.) Sew border strips in place; press seams toward borders.

Add Green Calligraphy inner border strips to long sides of table runner.

4. Using an acrylic ruler and rotary cutter – and aligning the 45° line on the ruler with the long edge of the table runner, and also aligning the long edge of the ruler with the edge of the rectangle as shown – trim the overhanging ends of each border strip.

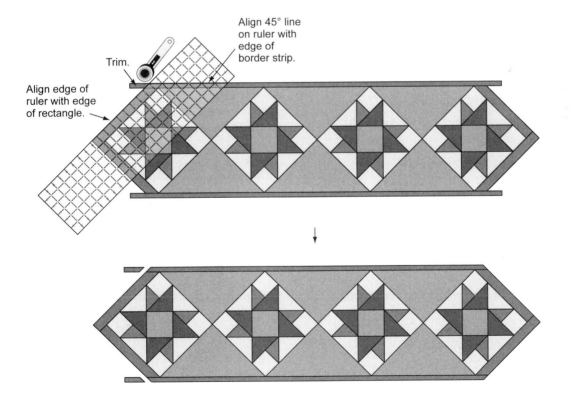

5. Repeat Steps 1-2 on page 10, this time adding the Red Filigree 1½" x 10" rectangles and the Red Filigree 1½" x 11" rectangles. Press seams toward rectangles just added. Using acrylic ruler and rotary cutter, trim the overhanging end of each rectangle.

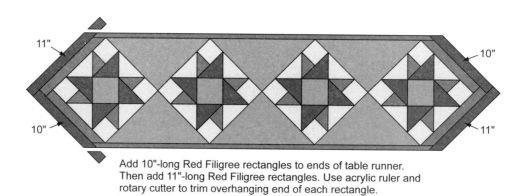

Add 10"-long Red Filigree rectangles to ends of table runner.
Then add 11"-long Red Filigree rectangles. Use acrylic ruler and
rotary cutter to trim overhanging end of each rectangle.

6. Repeat Steps 3-4 on page 11, this time adding Red Filigree 1" x 40" outer border strips to each long side of the table runner. Press seams toward outer borders. Using acrylic ruler and rotary cutter, trim the overhanging ends of each border strip.

Add Red Filigree outer border strips to long sides of table runner.
Using acrylic ruler and rotary cutter, trim the overhanging ends of
each border strip.

Finishing

Layer table runner, batting, and backing. Quilt as desired. Sew binding using your favorite method.

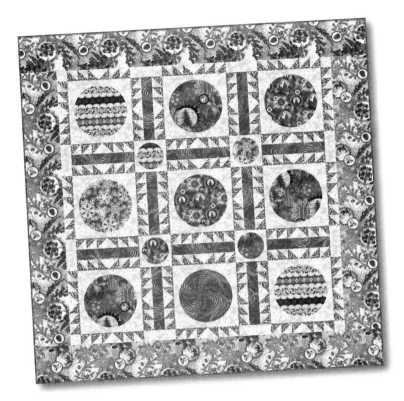

GLOBES

I think we all have our favorite holiday decorations. This quilt is a celebration of the beauty of ornaments. The large circles work well to show off your favorite fabrics and could be further embellished to add even more holiday charm.

Finished Quilt Size: 66½" x 66½"

Finished Block Sizes:
   12" x 12" (Large Globe Block)
   6" x 6" (Small Globe Block)

See this quilt in color in the center section of the book.

Materials

Fabric requirements are based on 40" fabric width.

- 2⅜ yds. White Snowflake (8WG4) for blocks and sashing
- ⅜ yd. Red Lace Stripe (3WGB1) for blocks
- ⅜ yd. Red Large Spheres (1WG1) for blocks
- ⅜ yd. Red Small Spheres (2WGB1) for blocks
- ⅜ yd. Red Snowflakes (8WG1) for blocks
- 1⅓ yds. Red Calligraphy (5FG21) for blocks, sashing, and binding
- 1 yd. Green Filigree (4WGB3) for sashing
- 2⅛ yds. Red Holly Collage (1WGB1) for border
- 4⅜ yds. for backing

Directions

All cutting measurements include ¼"-wide seam allowance. Unless otherwise indicated, cut strips across fabric width. Press seams in direction of arrows unless otherwise instructed.

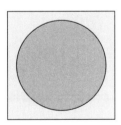

Large Globe Block   Small Globe Block   Sashing Unit

Cutting

Important note: *For this quilt, circles will be appliquéd to squares to make the Large and Small Globe blocks. In the cutting instructions below, the measurements given for cutting the circles <u>do not include seam allowance</u>. If you are using a fusible appliqué technique, follow the fusing and cutting instructions given on your fusible product. If you are using a traditional, hand-sewn, appliqué technique, you will need to add seam allowance to the measurements given below. Make cutting templates for the large and small circles, using thin cardboard or template plastic. Draw circles onto your template material, using a compass, or by tracing around appropriately-sized plates.*

From White Snowflake, cut:
- 9 squares, 12½" x 12½", for blocks
- 4 squares, 6½" x 6½", for blocks
- 9 squares, 5¼" x 5¼"; cut each square twice diagonally to make 36 large triangles for sashing
- 72 squares, 2⅞" x 2⅞"; cut each square once diagonally to make 144 small triangles for sashing
- 8 rectangles, 2½" x 6½", for sashing
- 4 squares, 2½" x 2½", for cornerstones

From Red Lace Stripe, cut:
- 2 large circles, 10" diameter
- 1 small circle, 5" diameter

From Red Large Spheres, cut:
- 3 large circles, 10" diameter
- 1 small circle, 5" diameter

From Red Small Spheres, cut:
- 2 large circles, 10" diameter
- 1 small circle, 5" diameter

From Red Snowflakes, cut:
- 1 large circle, 10" diameter
- 1 small circle, 5" diameter

From Red Calligraphy, cut <u>in order given</u>:
- 8 strips, 2½" x 40", for double-fold binding
- 1 large circle, 10" diameter
- 12 rectangles, 2½" x 12½", for sashing

From Green Filigree, cut:
- 108 squares, 2⅞" x 2⅞"; cut each square once diagonally to make 216 small triangles for sashing

From Red Holly Collage, cut:
- 4 strips, 7½" x length of fabric, for outer border (Strips are cut long, and will be trimmed later.)

Block Assembly

1. Using your favorite appliqué technique, appliqué an assorted-print 10" circle to a White Snowflake 12½" square as shown. Repeat to make a total of 9 Large Globe blocks.

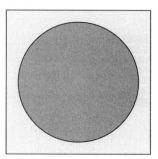

Make 9.

2. Appliqué an assorted-print 5" circle to a White Snowflake 6½" square as shown. Repeat to make a total of 4 Small Globe blocks.

Make 4.

3. Using 6 Green Filigree small triangles, 4 White Snowflake small triangles, and 1 White Snowflake large triangle, assemble a triangle unit as shown. Repeat to make a total of 36 units.

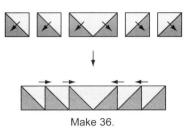

Make 36.

4. Using 2 triangle units from Step 3, and 1 Red Calligraphy 2½" x 12½" rectangle, assemble a sashing unit as shown. Repeat to make a total of 12 units.

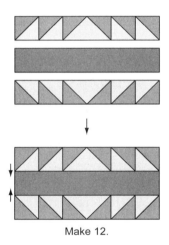

Make 12.

Quilt Top Assembly

1. Sew together in a horizontal row: 3 Large Globe blocks, 2 sashing units, and 2 triangle units. Repeat to make a total of 3 rows.

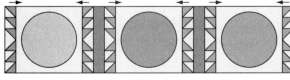

Make 3.

2. Sew together in a horizontal row: 2 Small Globe blocks, 3 sashing units, and 2 White Snowflake 2½" x 6½" rectangles. Repeat to make a total of 2 rows.

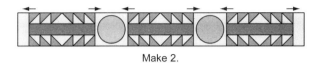

Make 2.

3. Sew together in a horizontal row: 3 triangle units, 2 White Snowflake 2½" x 6½" rectangles, and 2 White Snowflake 2½" squares. Repeat to make a total of 2 rows.

Make 2.

4. Sew rows, from Steps 1-3, together as shown below.

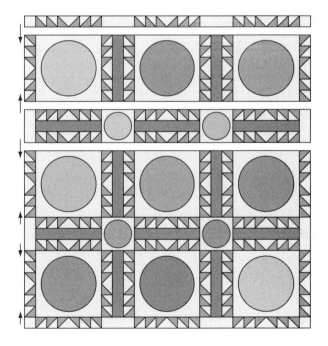

Borders

1. Measure length of quilt top through center. Trim 2 Red Holly Collage outer border strips to this measurement, and sew to sides of quilt as shown in the Quilt Assembly Diagram below. Press seams toward outer borders.

2. Measure width of quilt top, including borders just added, through center. Trim remaining 2 Red Holly Collage outer border strips to this measurement, and sew to top and bottom of quilt. Press seams toward outer borders.

Finishing

Layer quilt top, batting, and backing. Quilt as desired. Sew binding using your favorite method. Don't forget to sign and date your finished quilt.

Quilt Assembly Diagram

Globes

Table Runner

Holiday Harlequin

Crystal Blue

CRYSTAL BLUE

I think this quilt really captures the beauty of a snow-covered world. The pattern has a light airy feeling to it, and the combination of the whites in the prints, plus the different blues, gives it a cool, crisp feel.

Finished Quilt Size: 77½" x 77½"

Finished Block Size: 30" x 30"

See this quilt in color in the center section of the book.

Materials

Fabric requirements are based on 40" fabric width.

- 5 yds. White Snowflake (8WG4) for blocks and sashing
- 1⅓ yds. Dark Blue Snowflake (8WG2) for blocks
- 1⅓ yds. Blue Large Spheres (1WG2) for blocks and cornerstones
- ⅞ yd. Blue Calligraphy (5FG22) for blocks
- 1⅓ yds. Light Blue Snowflake (8WG5) for blocks
- 1⅛ yds. Blue Filigree (4WGB2) for inner border and binding
- 2⅜ yds. Blue Holly Collage (1WGB2) for outer border
- 5 yds. for backing

Directions

All cutting measurements include ¼"-wide seam allowance. Unless otherwise indicated, cut strips across fabric width. Press seams in direction of arrows unless otherwise instructed.

Important note: Foundation-piecing, as well as traditional piecing, is used to construct the blocks for this quilt. You'll find the necessary paper foundations, as well as foundation piecing instructions, on pages 25-28. (There are 3 different foundations needed for each block.) Make 17 photocopies of Foundation A, and 33 copies each of Foundations B and C (the one extra copy of each foundation will be used to make cutting templates).

Pieced Block

Cutting

From White Snowflake, cut:

- 12 strips, 2½" x 30½", for sashing
- From the remainder of the White Snowflake fabric, you will be cutting shapes to use for foundation piecing the blocks. Cut apart one photocopy each of Foundation A, Foundation B, and Foundation C so that you have a paper template of each background piece. (All of the background pieces are shown in white in the diagram below, and all of the background pieces will be cut from your White Snowflake fabric.)

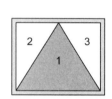

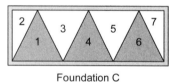

Foundation B

Foundation C

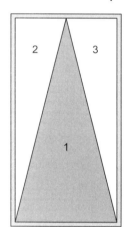

Foundation A

Cut a background piece by pinning a *right-side-up* template on the *wrong side* of your fabric as shown below. With scissors or rotary cutter, cut around the template leaving a ⅜"-½" seam allowance on all sides. You can cut more than one background piece at a time, by stacking fabric 4-8 layers deep (making sure that each fabric layer is *wrong-side-up,* and securing layers with several pins), then positioning your paper template, and cutting as described above.

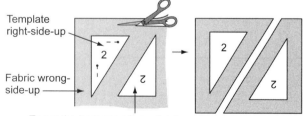

Template right-side-up

Fabric wrong-side-up

To get the best use of your fabric, rotate and "nest" template (still right-side-up).

From White Snowflake, (continued):

For Foundation A, cut:
- 16 of piece #2
- 16 of piece #3

For Foundation B, cut:
- 32 of piece #2
- 32 of piece #3

For Foundation C, cut:
- 32 of piece #2
- 32 of piece #3
- 32 of piece #5
- 32 of piece #7

From Dark Blue Snowflake:

- (Follow general foundation-piecing cutting instructions given at left.)
  For Foundation A, cut:
  - 16 of piece #1

From Blue Large Spheres, cut:

- 4 squares, 6½" x 6½", for blocks
- 16 squares, 5½" x 5½", for blocks
- 16 squares, 4½" x 4½", for blocks
- 16 squares, 3½" x 3½", for blocks
- 9 squares, 2½" x 2½", for cornerstones

From Blue Calligraphy:

- (Follow general foundation-piecing cutting instructions given at left.)
  For Foundation B, cut:
  - 32 of piece #1

From Light Blue Snowflake:

- (Follow general foundation-piecing cutting instructions given at left.)
  For Foundation C, cut:
  - 32 of piece #1
  - 32 of piece #4
  - 32 of piece #6

From Blue Filigree, cut:

- 9 strips, 2½" x 40", for double-fold binding
- 7 strips, 1½" x 40", for inner border

From Blue Holly Collage, cut:

- 4 strips, 5" x length of fabric, for outer border (Strips are cut long, and will be trimmed later.)

Block Assembly

1. Following general foundation piecing instructions on pages 25-28, piece and trim 16 Foundation A units, 32 Foundation B units, and 32 Foundation C units.

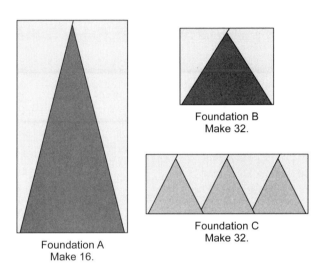

Foundation A
Make 16.

Foundation B
Make 32.

Foundation C
Make 32.

2. Using 2 Foundation B units, 2 Foundation C units, 1 Blue Large Spheres 5½" square, 1 Blue Large Spheres 4½" square, and 1 Blue Large Spheres 3½" square, assemble a block corner unit as shown. Repeat to make a total of 16 units.

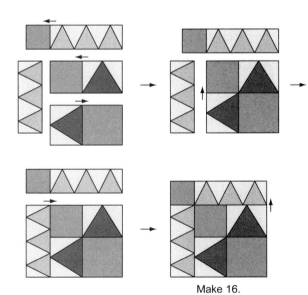

Make 16.

3. Using 4 block corner units, 4 Foundation A units, and 1 Blue Large Spheres 6½" square, assemble a block as shown. Repeat to make a total of 4 blocks.

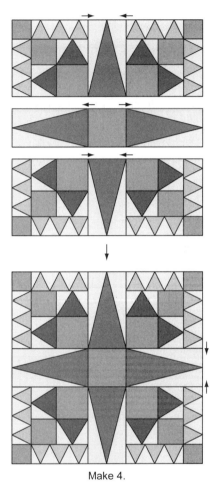

Make 4.

Quilt Top Assembly

1. Sew 2 blocks and 3 White Snowflake 2½" x 30½" sashing strips together in a horizontal row as shown. Repeat to make a total of 2 rows.

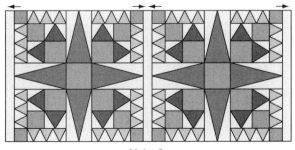

Make 2.

2. Sew 2 White Snowflake 2½" x 30½" sashing strips and 3 Blue Large Spheres 2½" squares together in a horizontal row as shown. Repeat to make a total of 3 rows.

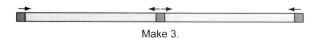

Make 3.

3. Sew rows, from Steps 1 and 2, together as shown in the Quilt Assembly Diagram below. Press seams away from block-rows.

Borders

1. Sew the 7 Blue Filigree 1½" x 40" inner border strips together, end-to-end, to make one long strip. Press seams open.

2. Measure length of quilt top through center. From the Blue Filigree long strip, cut 2 inner border strips to this measurement, and sew to sides of quilt. Press seams toward borders.

3. Measure width of quilt top, including borders just added, through center. From the Blue Filigree long strip, cut 2 inner border strips to this measurement, and sew to top and bottom of quilt. Press seams toward borders.

4. Measure length of quilt top through center. Trim 2 Blue Holly Collage outer border strips to this measurement, and sew to sides of quilt. Press seams toward outer borders.

5. Measure width of quilt top, including borders just added, through center. Trim remaining 2 Blue Holly Collage outer border strips to this measurement, and sew to top and bottom of quilt. Press seams toward outer borders.

Finishing

Layer quilt top, batting, and backing. Quilt as desired. Sew binding using your favorite method. Don't forget to sign and date your finished quilt.

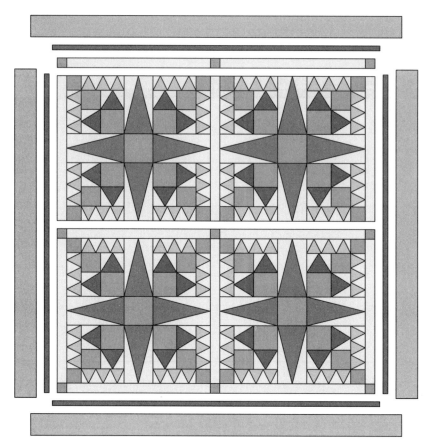

Quilt Assembly Diagram

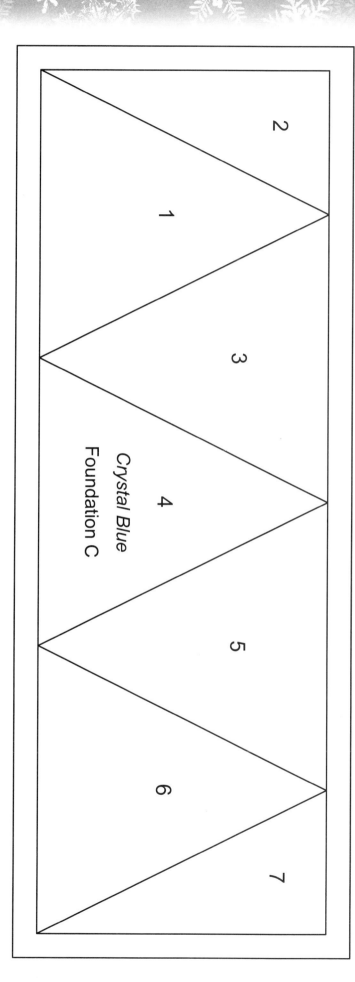

Crystal Blue
Foundation C

2

1

3

4

5

6

7

Foundation Paper Piecing

The foundations needed for the Crystal Blue quilt are on pages 25-28. Foundation paper piecing might look a little complicated at first but, once learned, it's a very easy technique. If this is your first experience with foundation paper piecing, keep these tips in mind:

- Be sure to sew the pieces down in the numbered sequence.
- Always add the fabric to the unmarked side of the paper foundation.
- Sew on the marked lines, using a short (approximately 16 stitches per inch) stitch length. Begin sewing a few stitches before the outer marked line, and end sewing a few stitches past the marked line (see illustration #3 on page 27).
- Whenever possible, plan placement of your fabric pieces so that the straight of grain runs either vertically or horizontally in your block.

When you're ready to begin:

1. Arrange your first piece of fabric, right side up, on the unmarked side of the photocopied foundation, so that it entirely covers the space marked "1" as shown below. You may want to hold your foundation and fabric up to a light to make sure that coverage is complete. Always aim to leave a seam allowance of at least ¼" on all sides. Excess will be trimmed after sewing.

To start, place fabric right side up on the *unmarked side* of the photocopied foundation. Make sure that fabric completely covers the space marked "1".

Foundations

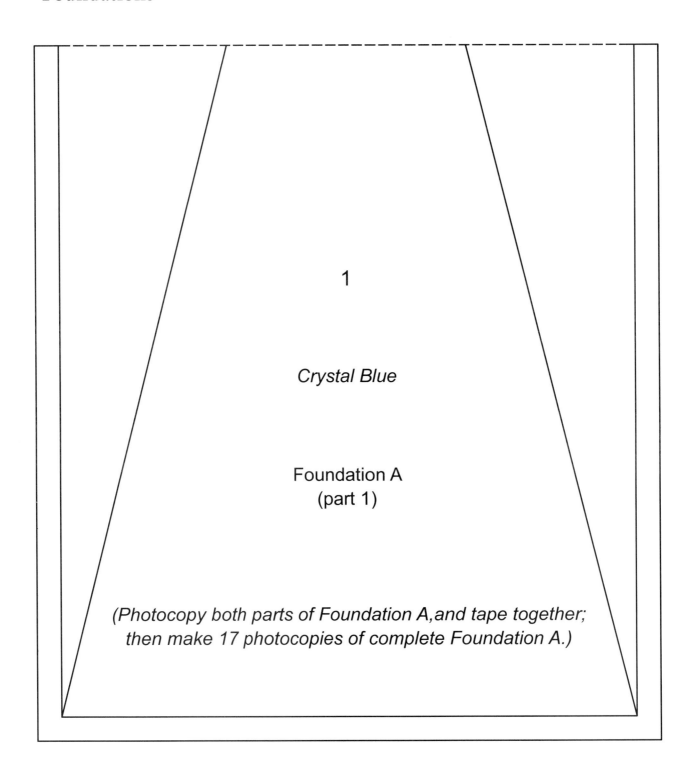

1

Crystal Blue

Foundation A
(part 1)

*(Photocopy both parts of Foundation A, and tape together;
then make 17 photocopies of complete Foundation A.)*

Foundation Paper Piecing *(continued)*

2. Pin the first piece in place on the foundation as shown below.

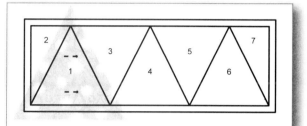

The fabric for space #1 is shown underneath the foundation, pinned into place. (The foundation is shown semi-transparent, so the fabric beneath can be seen.)

3. Lay the #2 piece of fabric, right sides together, on top of the #1 fabric. Pin in place, then flip foundation over, and sew on the line between #1 and #2 spaces.

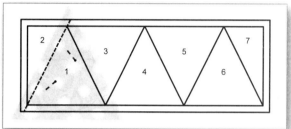

Add second fabric, and sew on the line between #1 and #2 spaces. (The foundation is shown semi-transparent, so the fabric beneath can be seen.)

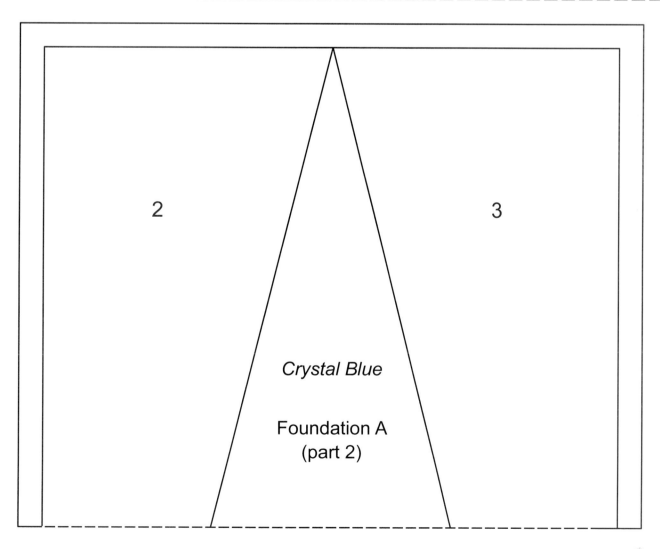

2

3

Crystal Blue

Foundation A
(part 2)

Foundation Paper Piecing *(continued)*

4. Remove pins and turn foundation back to fabric side. Using scissors, trim seam allowance just sewn to ¼", and press #2 piece open.

Turn paper foundation over. Trim seam allowance of seam just sewn, and press #2 piece of fabric open.

5. Continue adding pieces following the general foundation piecing instructions in Steps 3 and 4, and following the numerical sequence

marked on each foundation. After the last piece has been stitched and pressed, use rotary cutter and ruler to trim the pieced unit at the marked edges of the paper foundation as shown below (cut through all layers: paper and fabric). Then, carefully remove paper from your pieced unit.

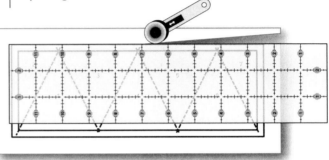

Use rotary cutter and ruler to trim the pieced unit along the outermost solid line of the paper foundation.

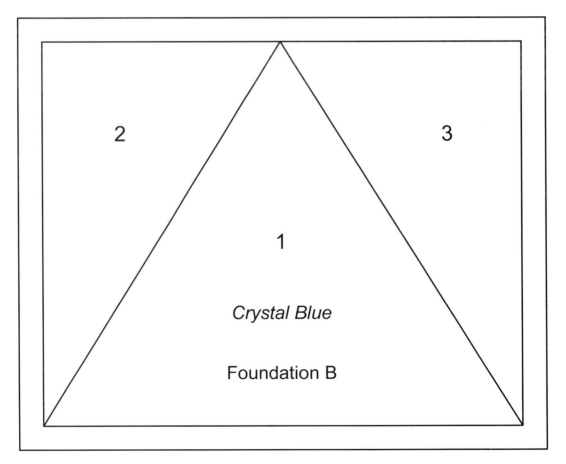

2

3

1

Crystal Blue

Foundation B

HOLIDAY HARLEQUIN

I really like the simplicity and graphic boldness of this pattern. This is one of those quilts that would look great draped over your couch, or it could also make a really cool table covering.

Finished Quilt Size: 44" x 56"

Finished Diamond Size: 4" x 6"

See this quilt in color in the center section of the book.

Materials

Fabric requirements are based on 40" fabric width.

- 1½ yds. White Snowflake (8WG4) for diamonds and edge triangles
- ⅓ yd. Red Small Spheres (2WGB1) for diamonds
- ⅓ yd. Red Filigree (4WGB1) for diamonds
- ⅓ yd. Red Calligraphy (5FG21) for diamonds
- ⅓ yd. Red Large Spheres (1WG1) for diamonds
- ⅓ yd. Red Holly Collage (1WGB1) for diamonds
- ⅓ yd. Red Snowflake (8WG1) for diamonds
- ⅓ yd. Green Filigree (4WGB3) for diamonds
- 1 yd. Green Calligraphy (5FG24) for diamonds and binding
- 1⅞ yds. Red Lace Stripe (3WGB1) for diamonds and border
- 3¾ yds. for backing (lengthwise seam)

Directions

All cutting measurements include ¼"-wide seam allowance. Unless otherwise indicated, cut strips across fabric width. Press seams in direction of arrows unless otherwise instructed.

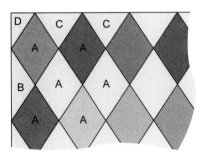

Cutting

Note: *Templates for this quilt are on page 31.*

From White Snowflake, cut:
- 56 diamonds (Template A)
- 14 triangles (Template B)
- 16 triangles (Template C)
- 2 triangles + 2 triangles reversed (Template D)

From each of Red Small Spheres, Red Filigree, Red Calligraphy, Red Large Spheres, Red Holly Collage, Red Snowflake, and Green Filigree, cut:

- 8 diamonds (Template A)

From Green Calligraphy, cut in order given:

- 6 strips, 2½" x 40", for double-fold binding
- 8 diamonds (Template A)

From Red Lace Stripe, cut in order given:

- 4 strips, 4¼" x length of fabric, for border (*Note:* Selectively cut border strips so that the design is the same in each strip, as shown in the photo in the center section of the book; this will make the design match at the mitered corners.)
- 8 diamonds (Template A)

Quilt Top Assembly

1. After referring to the photo in the center section of the book for fabric placement, sew Template A diamonds, Template B triangles, and Template C triangles together in diagonal rows as shown in the Quilt Assembly Diagram below. Press seams away from White Snowflake pieces.

2. Sew diagonal rows together; press seams in one direction. Add Template D triangles to corners of quilt top. Press seams toward D triangles.

Borders

Following the mitered border instructions on pages 6-7 (Steps 3-8), sew Red Lace Stripe border strips to quilt top.

Finishing

Layer quilt top, batting, and backing. Quilt as desired. Sew binding using your favorite method. Don't forget to sign and date your finished quilt.

Quilt Assembly Diagram

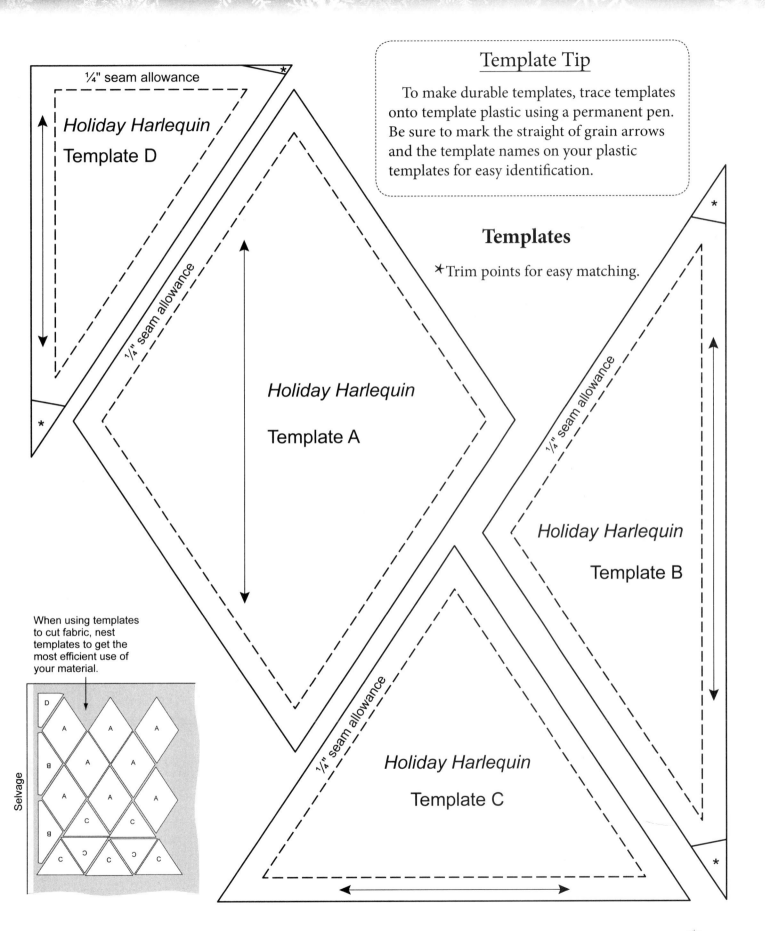

¼" seam allowance

Holiday Harlequin

Template D

¼" seam allowance

Holiday Harlequin

Template A

Template Tip

To make durable templates, trace templates onto template plastic using a permanent pen. Be sure to mark the straight of grain arrows and the template names on your plastic templates for easy identification.

Templates

*Trim points for easy matching.

¼" seam allowance

Holiday Harlequin

Template B

¼" seam allowance

Holiday Harlequin

Template C

When using templates to cut fabric, nest templates to get the most efficient use of your material.

Selvage

TREE SKIRT

This is a really easy-to-make tree skirt, and it looks beautiful when finished — you almost hate to cover it with presents. We have used all the same fabric for our diamonds, but it would also look nice using a variety of prints.

Finished Size: 82" diameter

See this tree skirt in color on the inside back cover.

Materials

Fabric requirements are based on 40" fabric width.

- 2 yds. Red Holly Collage (1WGB1) for diamonds
- 1⅞ yds. Red Lace Stripe (3WGB1) for border
- 4½ yds. for backing

Directions

All cutting measurements include ¼"-wide seam allowance. Press seams in direction of arrows unless otherwise instructed.

Important note: *You will need to make a template for the diamond shape used in the tree skirt. As shown in the illustration at right, start by drawing, with pencil and ruler, a 20" x 30" rectangle on a large sheet of paper. Mark the center point of each side of the rectangle then, with pencil and ruler, draw lines from one center point to the next, making a diamond. Using an acrylic ruler, draw a straight line three inches from one tip of the diamond as shown. Cut out your paper template.*

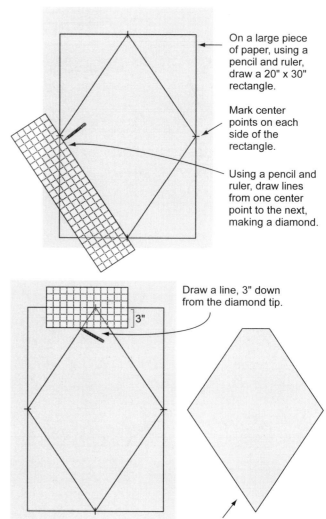

On a large piece of paper, using a pencil and ruler, draw a 20" x 30" rectangle.

Mark center points on each side of the rectangle.

Using a pencil and ruler, draw lines from one center point to the next, making a diamond.

Draw a line, 3" down from the diamond tip.

Cut out paper template.

Cutting

From Red Holly Collage, cut:

- 5 diamonds (*Note:* Use paper template – see template directions on page 32 – and arrange template as shown at right to get best use of fabric.)

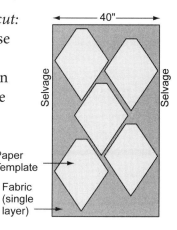

40"

Selvage

Selvage

Paper Template

Fabric (single layer)

From Red Lace Stripe, cut:

- 5 strips, 6¾" x length of fabric, for border (*Note:* Selectively cut border strips so that the design is the same in each strip, as shown in photo on the inside back cover; this will make the design match at the mitered corners. After cutting the 5 strips, cut each strip in half to make 10 strips, each 6¾" x approx. 30" long.)

Diamond Assembly

1. At tip of each Red Holly Collage diamond, with fabric right-side-up, using a pencil and ruler, lightly mark 2 short lines, each ¼" from fabric edge as shown below. The pencil lines will intersect near the tip of the diamond: this point of intersection will be important in the next step.

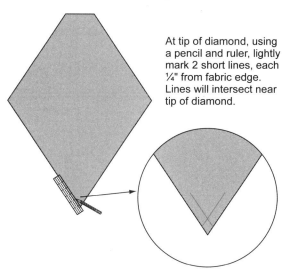

At tip of diamond, using a pencil and ruler, lightly mark 2 short lines, each ¼" from fabric edge. Lines will intersect near tip of diamond.

2. With right sides together, pin and sew a Red Lace Stripe 6¾" x 30" border strip to a Red Holly Collage diamond. Start stitching at the tip of the diamond, where the drawn lines intersect. Back-stitch to secure. Press seam toward border strip.

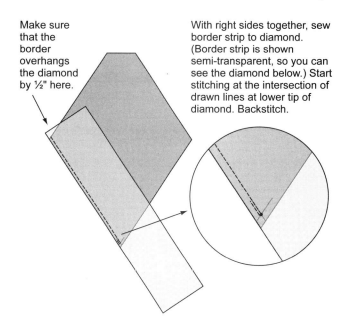

Make sure that the border overhangs the diamond by ½" here.

With right sides together, sew border strip to diamond. (Border strip is shown semi-transparent, so you can see the diamond below.) Start stitching at the intersection of drawn lines at lower tip of diamond. Backstitch.

3. With right sides together, pin and sew a 2nd Red Lace Stripe 6¾" x 30" border strip to the unit made in Step 2. End stitching at the tip of the diamond, where the drawn lines intersect. Back-stitch to secure. Press seam toward border strip.

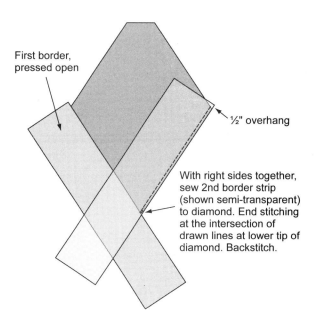

First border, pressed open

½" overhang

With right sides together, sew 2nd border strip (shown semi-transparent) to diamond. End stitching at the intersection of drawn lines at lower tip of diamond. Backstitch.

4. Trim excess from upper portion of border strips by aligning an acrylic ruler with edges of diamond as shown, and trimming with rotary cutter. *Do not trim lower portion of border strips.*

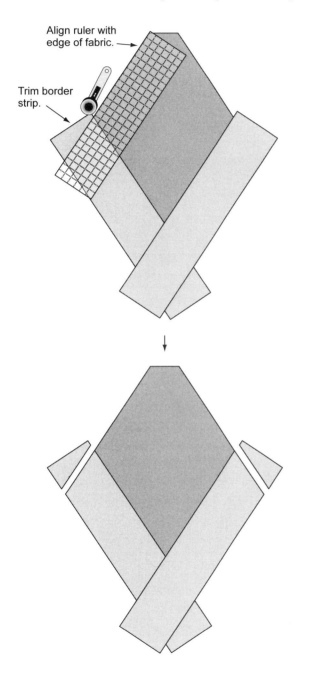

Align ruler with edge of fabric.

Trim border strip.

5. Working on a table, fold diamond unit in half lengthwise, so that borders are aligned with right sides together and raw edges even. (For this step, fold the pressed seam allowances back toward

the diamond.) Pin borders together as shown. Align an acrylic ruler with the folded edge of the diamond and, with a sharp pencil draw a line on the wrong side of border. Begin drawing line at end of stitching.

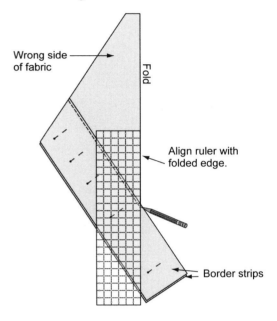

Wrong side of fabric

Fold

Align ruler with folded edge.

Border strips

6. Pin over drawn line, through both borders, to secure; then stitch on the drawn line, beginning at inner corner with backstitch, and ending at border outer raw edges. Trim excess, leaving a ¼"-wide seam allowance.

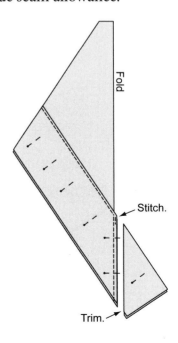

Fold

Stitch.

Trim.

7. Press corner seam open. Press border seams back toward borders.

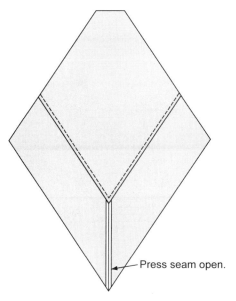

—Press seam open.

8. Repeat Steps 1-7 to make a total of 5 diamond units.

9. Using 1 of the diamond units – completed in Step 7 – as a template, trace and cut out 5 backing diamonds from your backing fabric.

Tree Skirt Assembly

1. With right sides together, and using ¼" seam allowance, sew the 5 diamond units together, as shown, to make the tree skirt top. Press seams open.

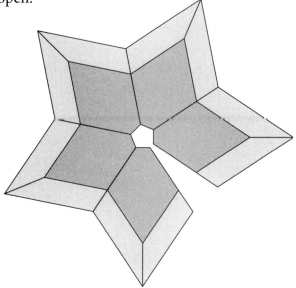

2. With right sides together, and using ¼" seam allowance, sew the 5 diamond backing units together, as shown, to make the tree skirt backing. Press seams open.

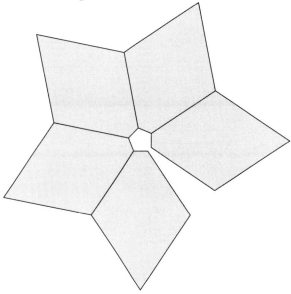

Finishing

1. With right sides together, pin and sew tree skirt top and backing together, leaving a 6" opening for turning. Backstitch to secure.

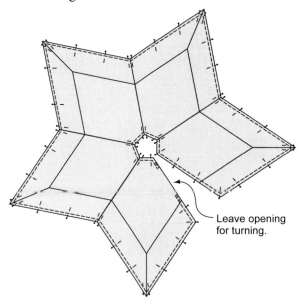

Leave opening for turning.

2. Turn tree skirt right side out. Press. Whipstitch opening closed. If desired, topstitch around edge of tree skirt.

Other Publications from In The Beginning Fabrics

- *Floragraphix IV Quilt Designs,*
  by Jason Yenter
- *Floragraphix III Quilt Designs,*
  by Jason Yenter
- *Floragraphix II Quilt Designs,*
  by Jason Yenter
- *Floragraphix I Quilt Designs,*
  by Jason Yenter
- *Bohemian Bedroom,* by Jason Yenter
- *Dancin' Teapot Quilt,*
  from In The Beginning Fabrics
- *Best of Blended Quilts,*
  by Marsha McCloskey and
  Sharon Evans Yenter
- *Blended Quilts II,* by Marsha McCloskey
- *Blended Wall Quilts,*
  by Sharon Evans Yenter
- *Playtime to Bedtime Quilts,*
  by Sharon Evans Yenter
- *Fat 8ths and Friends,*
  by Marsha McCloskey
- *More Fat 8ths and Friends,*
  by Marsha McCloskey
- *Garden Twist Quilts,*
  from In The Beginning Fabrics

Credits

Editor: Wendy Slotboom
Copy Editor: Laurie Shifrin
Illustrations and Book Design: Wendy Slotboom
Cover Design and Color Pages: Jason Yenter

Wintergraphix Quilt Designs
©2009 Jason Yenter
In The Beginning Quilts, Inc., Seattle, Washington USA

ISBN-13: 978-0-9791646-7-5
ISBN-10: 0-9791646-7-2
Printed in USA

About the Author

Jason Yenter has grown up in the quilting world ever since his mother, Sharon, opened In The Beginning Fabrics in 1977. Starting as a part-time stock boy in his early teens, he worked his way up through the company, and is now president and one of the company's designers. With his busy life he has very little time to quilt these days, but he truly enjoys designing fabrics and quilt patterns to inspire the creativity of others.

Jason lives in Seattle, Washington, with his crazy son Zack – they have a lot of fun.